Snorkel St. John

2010

2nd Edition

2013

Contact me at

burt.jill@ymail.com

SNORKEL ST. JOHN

JILL BURT

PHOTOGRAPHY

by JIM BURT

2013

With Special Thanks To

Bailey Carr

For Artistic Creativity

Above: School of Blue Tang

Page 2: View of Coral Bay

Opposite Page: View from Ram's Head

Foureye Butterflyfish Swimming Through Coral

CONTENTS

VIII. Snorkeling

Previous page: Parrotfish

Above: Flamingo Toungue

Long-Spined Sea Urchin

If you wish to snorkel from shore in tropical waters with coral reefs and colorful fish, St. John could be the place for you. This small, isolated island has numerous snorkeling sites off its shores. Several of the most enjoyable sites are described in this book with detailed directions for finding each. Many of the sites are in the Coral Bay region, which has no resorts, so you may find yourself exploring alone. The surf varies with the season and the wind, but there are

Above: Cushioned Sea Star

Opposite: Two snorkelers at a deserted beach

usually several sites with little or no surf for clear water and easy entry. No attempt has been made to include every beach and bay on this wonderful island. The places described here are the ones I feel have the best snorkeling. Enjoy!

II. DESCRIPTION

St. John, US Virgin Islands, is a small island of about 20 square miles. It is about 8 miles long and 3 miles wide, but it is so irregularly shaped that this may be misleading. It is a volcanic island, and thus it is mountainous with Bordeaux Mountain reaching 1277 feet. Driving on the island is like riding a roller coaster, with lots of ups and downs, twists and turns. Driving is on the left side of the road, and all of the vehicles have the steering wheel on the left side. Domestic animals run wild, and it is not unusual to see goats, sheep, burros and roosters in the road.

Population is around 5000, with most of these residing in Cruz Bay on the west end where the ferries arrive from St. Thomas. There is no airport on St. John and the ports are not deep enough for cruise ships. It is a popular place for

Above: School of French Grunts

Above: Sheep in the road

sailors, and the bays are usually full of anchored boats. The few resorts on this island are near Cruz Bay. The only other settlement of any note Bayis Coral is on the east side. A construction boom has increased the number of private homes, with many available for daily and weekly rental.

Top: Mountainous Coral Bay Road

Above:Papaya Tree above Coral Bay

14

Many beaches and bays ring the island and provide entry to a wonderland of snorkeling from shore. Numerous concessions offer snorkeling from boats and kayaks as well. Many of the beaches are within the boundaries of the Virgin Islands National Park, so it is rare to see beachfront homes. The desirable home locations are on the bluffs and mountainsides overlooking the bays.

Above: Coral Bay Views

III MAPS

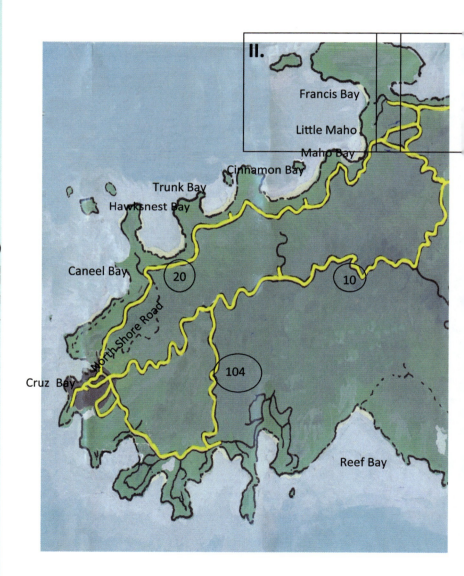

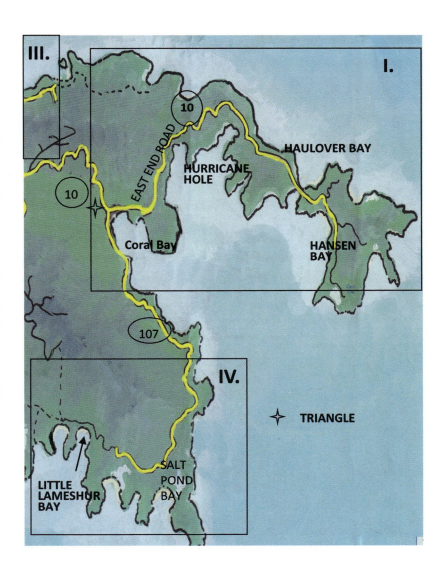

III.

I.

10

EAST END ROAD

HAULOVER BAY

**HURRICANE
HOLE**

10

Coral Bay

**HANSEN
BAY**

107

IV.

✦ **TRIANGLE**

SALT
POND
BAY

**LITTLE
LAMESHUR
BAY**

MAPS

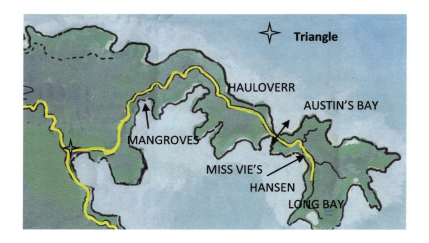

Map I. East End

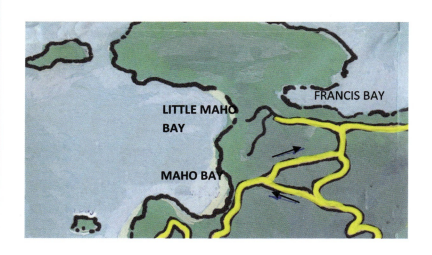

Map II. North Shore Beaches

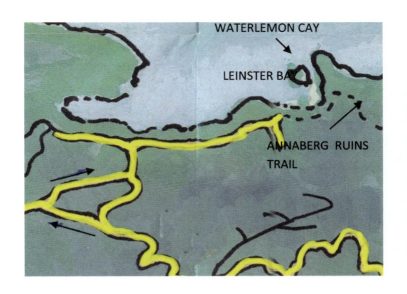

WATERLEMON CAY

LEINSTER BAY

ANNABERG RUINS
TRAIL

MAP III. Leinster Bay

LITTLE LAMESHUR
BAY

GROOTPAN
Bay

SALT POND
BAY

KIDDELL
BAY

MAP IV. Southeast Bays

Indians may have inhabited St John as early as 770 BC, but the earliest European settlements were in the 1720's. Several European countries became interested in cultivating sugar cane for profit about that time. Ownership was disputed between England and Denmark for some time, with England eventually relinquishing its claims. Over 100 cotton and sugar plantations covered the island in those days. So many slaves were brought to work the plantations that the slaves soon outnumbered the free men.

After slave revolts and significant bloodshed, the Danish Parliament abolished slavery in the Danish West Indies. A decline of the plantations and a drop of population followed. The plantation of Carolina Estate in Coral Bay was kept running the longest. Planters finally abandoned the island and former slaves moved onto the land becoming land owners through various means. The inhabitants lived off the sea and subsistence farming of the land.

In 1917 the United States bought St. John from Denmark. News of the pristine island began to spread, and the tourist boom began. Laurence Rockefeller bought up much of the island, and in 1956, he donated 5000 acres to the United

Opposite: Plantation Ruins

Above: Modern Homes

States Federal Government to establish a National Park. Since then additional donations have been made, and the Virgin Islands National Park includes 7200 acres of land and 5600 acres underwater. About 60-70% of the island is protected as a National Park.

Above: View of Coral Bay

Opposite: Sunrise/Sunsets over Coral Bay

In a sentence, the weather is perfect. The temperature rarely gets above 85 degrees Fahrenheit or below 70 degrees. There is little humidity and a gentle sea breeze keeps life pleasant. The water temperature drops to about 79 degrees in the winter months and goes up to about 83 degrees in the summer. No wet suits are needed. Neoprene booties are recommended to protect the feet on some of the rocky shores. Rainstorms are rare. More rainfall occurs August to October than the remainder of the year. It may rain off and on for a day, and then be sunny the next day. Be thankful for the rainfall. Remember the cisterns are refilling, and most everyone is dependent on rainfall as the water source.

WEATHER

Opposite: After the rain

Above: A sunny day at Trunk Bay

VI. GETTING THERE AND AROUND

There is no airport on St. John. The nearest airport is the international airport on the nearby island of St. Thomas. When a plane arrives, the taxis line up at the airport exit to transport the tourists to the ferries and the local resorts. The cheapest taxi is one of the van shuttles that pack in 10-12 people. The closest ferry to St. John is only 1 mile away in the city of Charlotte Amalie. This is a pedestrian-only ferry which runs each way 3 times per day. Check online to see current ferry schedules. On the East end of the is-land is the town of Red Hook which has car/pedestrian fer-ry service to St. John every hour. The drive from the airport to Red Hook takes about 30 minutes.

Once you reach St. John, a rental car is the simplest form of transportation. If you stay in one of the resorts in Cruz Bay, you may be able to get by with taxi service. It is not uncommon to see one of the resort's taxis at the snorkeling spots around the island. If you opt for the rental car, you can rent on St. John or on St. Thomas and bring it over on the ferry. The rental cars on St. John are typically Jeep Wranglers with four-wheel drive. It is possible to encounter some roads where four-wheel drive is necessary, especially in case of rain.

Opposite: Car ferry to St. John

Top: Ferry terminal in Cruz Bay

Above: Pedestrians in Cruz Bay

Above: Rental jeeps parked at beach

There are a limited supply of cars on St. John, so be sure and reserve early. If you rent on St. Thomas, car rental is considerably cheaper. Be sure and specify four-wheel drive, or you may not get it. Now for the fun part... Bringing the rental car over on the ferry is one of those experiences of a lifetime. When you reach Red Hook, you will notice a parking lot of vehicles, with no apparent queue. You will also notice the cars are facing AWAY from the ferry harbor. That Is because you BACK onto the ferry. When loading begins, it seems that everyone begins backing toward the narrow ferry at one time. There is a ferryman who points when it is your turn to load. His job is to maximize the number of vehicles on each ferry, so you will be parking VERY close to your neighbors. The good news is that leaving the ferry is considerably less stressful, since you pull off frontward.

Don't forget driving is on the left side of the road. Roads are narrow, winding and have lots of ups and downs. Drive slowly and keep an eye out for those behind who want to go fast-

Above: Typical St. John road

Below: Car preparing to load ferry

er. Find a pull-out and let them pass until you feel comfortable driving here. There are two main roads across the island: center-line road, which takes you directly across the island from Cruz Bay to Coral Bay on the Eastern shore,

and North Shore Road which takes you along the North shore as the name suggests. Keep an eye out for animals of all sort, domestic and wild. Goats, sheep, burros and roosters are common in the road-ways.

Top: Burros in the road

Above: Market in Coral Bay

VII. VIRGIN ISLANDS NATIONAL PARK

The land that Rockefeller donated to the Federal Government became the nation's twenty-ninth National Park. Fred Seaton, Secretary of the Interior, promised the government would "take good and proper care of these precious acres and verdant hills and valleys and miles of sunny, sandy shores".   Other donations have increased the park size to 7200 acres of land and 5600 acres of underwater land. The underwater lands teem with marine life, and access to it is easy by snorkeling from shore.

In 2001 the Virgin Islands Coral Reef National Monument was established from federally owned submerged lands off the island of St. John. The coral reef and mangrove habitat are protected by the park service to maintain the biological diversity of the Caribbean.

The Visitor Center is at the harbor in Cruz Bay. Donations are accepted there, and Trunk Bay has an entrance fee, otherwise entrance to and exit from the park is seamless. The tourist would be unaware of the parklands except for the undeveloped acreage and lack of commercialization on the island. Remember to check by the Visitor Center for programs of interest, ranger-led hikes and naturalist talks.

Above: Protected seashore

Above Left: Bananaquits

Right: Antillean Crested Hummingbird

VIII. SNORKELING

Top: Queen Angelfish

Middle: Great Barracuda

Bottom: Peacock Flounder

Austin's Bay

Directions: From the intersection (the "triangle") of Centerline Road/Route 10 and Route 107, continue east on Route 10/East End Road. Continue down this road past where the national park ends—sign on right of road. Take the left on Defkreet Bay Road. Go to the first lookout on the left and park. Walk past the pullout and look for a grassy jeep trail on the left. Walk down this road to the bay.

This is a great entry to Haulover Bay north if the surf is up, because this entry is more protected. I have no idea what the official name of this bay is, but decided to name it for my oldest grandson, who discovered this bay with me. It is an easy , sandy entry. If the tide is in you can explore the mangroves to the right. Take the left around the point for some small coral heads and colorful fish.

Coral Heads

Grootpan Bay

Directions: From Cruz Bay take Centerline Road toward Coral Bay. At the intersection of Center Line Road, East End Road and Route 107, take Route 107 south. Continue through Coral Bay and all the way to the south end of the island. This route is several miles but the scenery and wildlife make it enjoyable. You will pass the Salt Pond parking lot. There are several signs here along with a bus stop. A few feet past this parking lot is another road—don't take it, keep going past the sign for Lameshur Cottages, then take the next left. You will be on a dirt road, but it is well maintained. Take the next left. Take a 3rd left at Mr. Wm Small 's lovely sign at the end of his driveway, saying "<—both bays ". Continue the main road, then take the next right. (If you miss this right, you will come out on Route 107, just south of Salt Pond.)

Stay on this road past 2 or 3 roads to the left and continue to the end of the road.

The shore of the bay is covered in small pebbles and larger rocks, which are uncomfortable on bare feet. The bay is large with clear water. It is off the beaten path and does not get a lot of traffic. The left side of the bay has very little coral growth, but has fair snorkeling. The far right can be magnificent with some large corals and some large fish. This is a favorite spot for scuba divers.

Hansen Bay

Hansen Bay is a large bay that includes several small bays that are good snorkeling areas. The last bay at the end of the road is called Long Bay as the far shore reaches out some distance into the water.

Directions: From the intersection (the triangle) of Centerline Road/Route 10 and Route 107, continue east on Route 10/East End Road. Continue down this road past Vie's Snack Shack on the left and Vie's Beach on the right. Go on to the next bay on the right.

Parking is somewhat limited but there is an effort to create a small parking lot across the road. The shore at this bay is rocky, but the entry is sandy and weed-covered. As always watch for urchins. Swim to the left and either go around the point and explore the rocky caverns and coral heads, or proceed out to the rock above the water to the right and beyond the left point.

If the long swim makes you uneasy, stick close to the left shore where the water is quite shallow. After a short distance coral begins to appear on the rocky shoreline. The corals are magnificent the further you go out, and the sea life is varied. If you are inspired, continue around the point to the next bay (Long Bay). You can take a break on the beach there before returning. Expect to see squid, sea turtles and a variety of fish. In the shallow weed beds, you

Above: Net fishing

Next pages: Sea Turtle and beach at Long Bay

may see seastars.

From time to time a floating bar comes into this bay and adventurous swimmers enjoy a swim out to the bar.

Haulover Bay

Directions: From Cruz Bay take Centerline Road (Route 10) to Coral Bay. At the intersection (the "triangle") of Route 107, Centerline Road and East End Road (Route 10 continued) take the East End Road. From Coral Bay, take the East End Road at the triangle. Stay on the East End Road until you see a sign indicating the end of the National Park.

Above: Haulover Bay North

This area gets its name from the narrow isthmus of land here. Boaters can haul boats from one bay to the other. Lore goes that pirates escaped capture here by hauling their boats from one bay to the other. The pursuers had boats too

Top: Haulover Bay North

Above: Foureye Butterflyfish

National Park Sign– Next stop– Haulover Bay

big to "haulover" and were forced to go all the way around east end in pursuit. Park along the side of the road. The bay immediately to the right is usually protected from the wind. There is a sandy beach with easy entry. The bottom is sandy and rocky. Swim to the far right where there is lots of coral and an abundance of fish. This is perhaps the easiest and most rewarding snorkeling for beginners.

Notice the direction of the wind. If it is from the south, go across the road and take the trail of about 5 min to the bay on the other side of East End. This bay is frequently affected by winter swells. If you catch it calm, by all means give it a try. Water entry is a little rocky, but worth the effort. Just watch out for urchins. Swim towards the left and enjoy the beautiful coral reefs and fish. The islands you see north of here are part of the British Virgin Islands.

Knobbed Porgy

and Tube Sponge

Kiddell Bay

Directions: From Cruz Bay take Center Line Road to Coral Bay. At the intersection of Center Line Road, East End Road and Route 107, take Route 107 south. Continue through Coral Bay and all the way to the south end of the island. This route is several miles but the scenery and wildlife make it enjoyable. You will pass the Salt Pond parking lot. There are several signs here along with a bus stop. A few feet past this parking lot is another road—don't take it, keep going past the sign for

Below: Common Octopus

Lameshur Cottages, then take the next left. You will be on a dirt road, but it is well maintained. Take the next left. Take a third left at Mr. Wm Small's lovely sign at the end of his driveway, saying "<—both bays " . Continue on the main road, then take the next right. (If you miss this right, you will come out on Route 107, just south of Salt Pond.) Take the next left all the way down to the bay.

The parking is in a small glade with a tire swing. The bay and the shoreline is covered in small cobblestones, so the water seems to be silt-free. It is usually very clear and visibility is great. The center of the bay is quite deep, 30 to 40 feet. Along the left shore, huge boulders have been pushed up leaving canyons which the fish and sea life love. If you swim to the mouth of the bay, there is a drop off to quite deep water and a wall of rock and coral. The clear water makes you feel you are in a fish bowl. Enjoy!

If you are hungry on the drive back north, you might stop at "Tourist Trap" near the Concordia camp sites. Enjoy outdoor eating and a delicious lunch. It is quite popular, so you may share a table.

Leinster Bay/ Waterlemon Cay

Directions: From Cruz Bay take the North Shore road across the island. Follow the signs to the Annaberg sugar mill ruins. From Coral Bay take the Centerline Road to the smoothie stand. Take a right at the sign to the North Shore road. Follow the signs to Annaberg as above. There is a nice parking lot for hiking to the ruins or the bay. From the parking lot, cross the road to the trailhead. This is a 1-mile, flat hike, which can be done in flip flops, but you may be more comfortable in walking or hiking shoes. There are lots of rocks on the trail. About 0.4 mi down the trail is a sand and rubble beach with good snorkeling. The entry is over rocks and coral, so watch for urchins and coral.

Above: Reef Squid

Above: Mongoose along trail to Waterlemon Cay

Right: Rock Beauty

Below: Sea Robin

Walk on another 0.5 miles or so to the wide sandy beach. The bottom here is grassy but it is common to see starfish (sea stars), reef squid and sting rays. If you are fortunate enough to see the reef squid, expect a delightful show. They seem to enjoy the attention and try to entertain with their military precision.

Continue on past the beach to the rocky shore near Waterlemon Cay. Entry is tricky with lots of rocks and urchins. Be careful! To the right is lots of coral and fish. The most popular snorkeling is out to the Cay and around to the far side. It is a long swim and not meant for beginners. The water is very clear and there is an

Below: Swimming to Waterlemon Cay

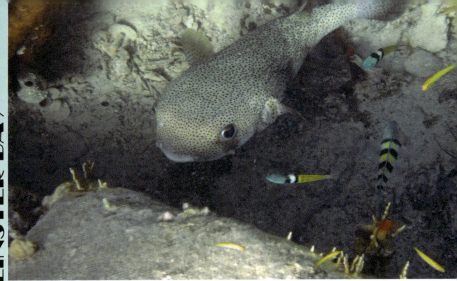

abundance of beautiful sea life. There can be current here, so always choose your path around the Cay to swim with the current. The water can be quite shallow on the left of the Cay and there is a small beach if you want a break.

Above:
Spotted
Spiny Puffer

Right:
Smooth
Trunkfish

48

Little Lameshur Bay

Above: Sign to Lameshur

Directions: From Cruz Bay take Centerline Road to Coral Bay. At the intersection of Centerline Road, East End Road and Route 107, take Route 107. This road goes all the way to the south end of the island. Enjoy the goats, burros, roosters, etc along the way. After several miles, the pavement ends. The dirt road is usually rough but passable. Proceed 1 mile on the dirt road to the 2nd bay. There is a nice parking area and bathroom facilities.

This is a popular location with a wide sandy beach and good

snorkeling. There are two choices here and both are recommended. Swim to the rocky left shore. There is an abundance of sea life and lots of coral. Nurse sharks have been reported here. They are quite safe. On the right there is a rock breaking through the water. Swim out to it .

Around that rock is more coral and lots of fish. Reef squid are sometimes here. As always keep your eye out for sea turtles.

Above: Little Lameshur Bay

Top: Rock in Lameshur Bay

Bottom: Reef Squid

Little Maho Bay

Directions: From Cruz Bay take the North Shore road across the island. Follow the signs to the Annaberg sugar mill ruins until you reach a fork with Francis Bay to the left and Annaberg to the right. Go left. Before reaching Francis Bay there is a sign for Little Maho Bay Camp. Take the left and follow this rough, narrow, dirt road to the camp. From Coral Bay take the Centerline Road to the smoothie stand. Take a right at the sign to the North Shore road.

Follow the signs to Annaberg and Little Maho Bay as above.

This camping site was scheduled for closure in May 2013. Park at the top of the hill, in the parking lot if possible, and, if not, alongside the road. Take the wooden walkway all the way down to the beach. It is a nice, sandy beach with easy entry. Swim along

Opposite: School of fish on Coral

Above: Beach at Little Maho

the rocky shore on either end of the beach. This bay lies between Maho and Francis, so you can swim around the point in either direction for good snorkeling..

Below: Colorful Coral

Bottom: End of Little Maho

Above: Christmas Tree Worms growing on Coral

Long Bay

Directions: From the intersection(the triangle) ofCenterline Road/Route 10 and Route 107, continue east on Route 10/East End Road. Continue on this road as far as it goes. There is a residential road to the left which passes Sloop Jones art shop. Stay to the right and park near the dumpster. Stay out of the private yard and walk along the path to the beach.

The shore is rocky, but if you go right you will find a small sandy beach. It is common to see men fishing with spears or nets in this bay. It is also a popular location for the kayak/snorkel vendors. They bring the kayakers to the rocks in the bay for snorkeling. The beach is usually quiet with few visitors. Enter the water from the sandy

SNORKELING

Above: School of Blue Tang

beach area, being careful to avoid the rocky shore on the far right and the urchins amid the rocks. Swim over the grassy, sandy bottom to the rocky spit on the right. The coral get more common as you swim further out. Approach the large rock from the right and circle it for some nice views. Give the large rock a wide berth on its left as the water gets quite shallow. Enjoy the coral canyons and variety of fish and sea turtles.

Maho Bay

Above: Maho Bay Beach

Directions: From Cruz Bay, take the North Shore road east. Just before it makes a turn back south, this will be the last bay on your left. From Coral Bay, take Centerline Road (Route 10) west. Watch for the Smoothie/Ice Cream stand on your left and take the immediate turn to the right – toward North Shore road. Stay left until you reach the first bay.

This is an easy bay to access as parking is close by on the roadside. It is a long bay with a wide sandy beach. As a result it is a very popular beach. It is sheltered and usually the calmest of the north shore beaches, and it is probably the best beach for children.

Entry into the water is easy. Look for sea turtles in the grassy bed. Swim to the right for the best snorkeling. The shore there is rocky and the snorkeling gets better and better as you go toward the point and beyond.

Above: Scrawled Filefish

Mangrove Snorkeling/ Princess Bay

Above: School of young Grunts

Snorkeling in mangroves has a bad rap, because mangroves usually grow in swamps. The water is usually
murky and uninviting. This area is fringe forest which
grows between a sheltered bay and hillsides. The water
is shallow, clear and warm. It feels like a large, fresh-

water pond. And it provides a unique snorkeling experience.

Directions: From the intersection(the "triangle") of Centerline Road/Route 10 and Route 107, continue east on Route 10/ East End Road.

Go past the Moravian Church and continue on for a couple of miles. The bay will come almost up to the road on the right. There is a cut through the mangrove which provides access. A couple of buoys are in the bay here for mooring small boats. There are a few parking spots just off the road here.

Enter the water through the cut in the mangroves. The

Below: Young barracuda

water will be very shallow and the bottom is grassy. Swim to your left and stay close to shore. This requires patience as you will be looking for very small creatures up under the mangrove roots. This is a nursery where the baby fish and other creatures are protected until they can go out on their own. Look for tiny corals, shell-fish, seahorses and tropical fish. Be careful not to touch the bottom and stir up the silt. The longer you stay, the more you will become proficient at spotting the small creatures. It is not something you will want to repeat

Below: Shellfish bed

Above: Young Butterfly Fish

everyday, but it is a very rewarding experience. It is equally enjoyable for all level of snorkelers.

Miss Vie's

Above: Vie's Snack Shack

This is a private beach with chaise lounges and nice snorkeling. It is open Tuesday through Saturday from 10 AM to 5 PM. Food is also available.

Directions: From the intersection(the "triangle") of Centerline Road/Route 10 and Route 107, continue east on Route 10/ East End Road. Stay on this road past the end of the National Park sign. Shortly on the left you will see Vie's Shack. The beach entry is across the road. You can pay at Vie's shack ($2.50 per person) or place your money in the slot at the entry.

Stop and have lunch at the shack. The food is delicious with local flavor. Enjoy fried garlic chicken with Johnny cakes and honey and/or conch fritters with salsa. There are hotdogs for the kids and a variety of soda and beer are available. Share the picnic tables around the shack with the other tourists.

The beach is wide with palm trees and assorted vegetation for shade. If you don't have your own chairs, kick back in one of Vie's. There is easy entry into the surf for snorkeling. Head for the rocks on the right where you will find a coral reef and lots of fish. If you need toilet facilities, check out the "outhouse" with the traditional half-moon on the door.

Below: Eating Area

Top: Red coral
Above: Facing a School of Bar Jacks

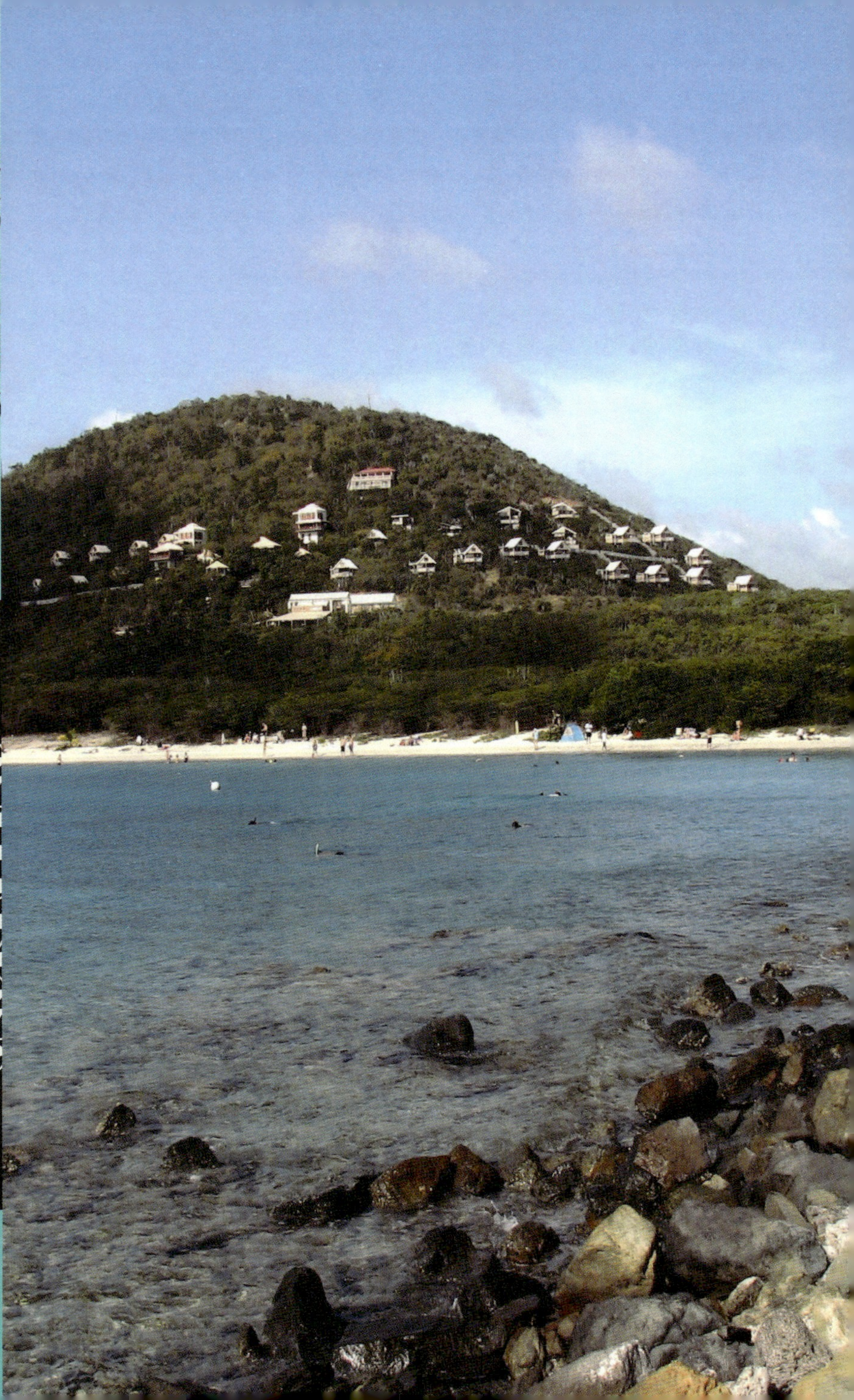

Salt Pond

Directions: From Cruz Bay take Centerline Road to Coral Bay. At the intersection of Centerline Road, East End Road and Routh 107, take Route 107. This road goes all the way to the south end of the island. The drive is several miles, but quite scenic with numerous bays along the left and local wildlife along the road. Shortly before the pavement ends you will see the parking at Salt Pond Bay. There are numerous signs here as well as a bus stop and a toilet.

Opposite: View of Salt Pond from Hiking Trail

Below: Trunkfish

Above:School of Cleaner Gobys

The walk to the bay is about 0.5 miles. It is downhill –
going in! This is another wide beach area that is quite
popular, even though there is not as much sand as some
other beaches. Again there are 2 choices for snorkeling.
Swim left along the rocky shore for clear water and an
abundance of fish. Viewing gets better the further you
swim. If you are a strong swimmer, you may want to try
swimming out to the jagged rocks that break the water
in the right of the bay. There is an assortment of fish
and coral here.

There are also some beautiful views from this area if you are interested in hiking. You can take a short trail from the far end of the beach for 0.3 miles to the Drunkard's Bay overlook where the surf is usually spectacular. You can also take a 1 mile trail from the far end of the beach to Ram's Head Overlook. Both of these require walking/hiking shoes. Ram's Head trail has a few steep portions. The views are magnifi-

Above: Under Water scene

cent. There are lots of cactus on this trail. Try to catch them in bloom in the spring.

Midway on the Ram's Head Trail is a rocky beach of blue cobblestone. If the surf is down, there is good snorkeling from this beach. If not, stop and listen to the surf return to sea through the blue cobblestones. It sounds much like wind chimes.

Below: Looking out at Salt Pond